Test Your Dog 2
GENIUS EDITION

RACHEL FEDERMAN
ILLUSTRATIONS BY
CHUCK GONZALES

HARPER

To Sky,
for a depth of loyalty I thought existed
only in myths and fairy tales.

HarperCollins*Publishers*
1 London Bridge Street
London SE1 9GF
www.harpercollins.co.uk

First published by HarperCollins*Publishers* in 2015

3 5 7 9 10 8 6 4 2

Text copyright © 2015 Rachel Federman
Illustrations by Chuck Gonzales
Cover and interior design: Rosamund Saunders
Cover images © Shutterstock

A catalogue record for this book is available from the British Library

ISBN 978-0-00-794928-1

Printed and bound in the UK

MIX
Paper from
responsible sources
FSC™ C007454

FSC™ is a non-profit international organisation established to promote the responsible
management of the world's forests. Products carrying the FSC label are independently certified
to assure consumers that they come from forests that are managed to meet the social, economic
and ecological needs of present and future generations.

Contents

Introduction   5

Chapter One: Daily Routine   9

Chapter Two: The Dog About Town   24

Chapter Three: Pitch-In Pup   43

Chapter Four: Holiday Hound   51

Chapter Five: Do You Speak Dog?   69

Chapter Six: Test Your Owner   89

The Activity Exam   99

Analysing Your Dog's Score   116

The General Certificate of Canine Excellence   128

Introduction

You know your dog can sit, fetch and roll over. But can he sit like a human? Respond to commands in multiple languages? Roll a die? Help you with a crossword puzzle? Appreciate Mozart? For this, the genius edition, we are going to take things up a notch. Think about the kind of dog whose aptitude lands it in the news, like the Labrador Bullmastiff in Seattle who regularly takes the bus to the park by herself. (Don't try this at home.) We don't want to know if your dog is simply well accommodated to life as your companion; we want to know if he could navigate the world without you. We know your dog is smart, but do you have a canine whiz on your hands?

To help you find out, I've loaded this book with quizzes that ask you to imagine your dog in various situations, and activity tests for you to perform with your dog. You'll also find hints and tips to boost your dog's brainpower. These activities might not get your four-legged friend into the college of her choice, but they will give you another way to bond with your pup, besides the eight hours you spend snuggling in bed, the four hours you spend snuggling on the couch, the many

walks you take together every day, and, of course, the long, drawn-out celebratory hugs that happen every time you reunite after an hour apart. Hopefully the results will increase your bragging rights to friends and family, put an extra bit of swagger in your tail-wagger, and lend weight to your not-so-secret conviction that your pup is superior to the rest of the neighbourhood dogs.

We know that intelligence tests for humans don't assess raw intelligence, but one that is context-dependent, aiming

to determine an individual's ability to succeed in the modern developed world. And even then, most tests don't always work well. Not least among the criticisms of today's testing culture is the fact that tests aren't a good predictor of future success: we all know someone who regularly did poorly on every test they were given as a child and whose career now outshines our own.

In the genius edition I've refined the approach to do the canine equivalent of separating the men from the boys (dogs from the pups?). Many of the skills tested aren't necessarily those a dog would need to succeed or to flourish. A dog who can conduct higher order reasoning and engage in rigorous critical thinking may not fare any better day to day at the park than his birdbrained pal – but he'll learn faster, understand you better, and might even enjoy a reading of Shakespeare or a trip to a modern art gallery if only he'd be allowed in.

For the first five sections, you don't have to conduct any trials. Simply pick the best answer from the choices given; nobody knows your dog like you do. For the sixth section you'll rely on your dog's expertise, and the activity tests you'll do with your dog. Keep a note of your answers and check your scores on pages 116–117 once you've finished all the sections.

Chapter One

DAILY ROUTINE

Dogs love routine and they hold us to those we establish (as many a Sunday morning hungover dog owner will tell you). How they respond to routine – and changes in it – can help us interpret their self-awareness, understanding of their environment and capacity for learning.

1. Does your dog have a sense of routine? Does she head to the door when it's time for her walk, head to her bowl when you usually feed her, expect your car to pull in at a certain time every day, and so on?

☐ No **NIL POINTS**

☐ Yes, but she's on holiday time (always two hours late, but ready to party) **1 POINT**

☐ Yes **2 POINTS**

2. How likely is your dog to repeat behaviour that is met with a negative reaction, such as jumping up on your legs?

☐ No cues seem to help; pretty much every greeting pins me to the ground **NIL POINTS**

☐ A subtle reminder each time does the trick **1 POINT**

☐ I snapped at her once and she's never done it again **2 POINTS**

3. If you forget your bag as you leave a park bench, what will your dog do?

☐ Did somebody say squirrels? **NIL POINTS**

☐ Bark in a seemingly random way until you figure out what the bark means **1 POINT**

☐ Grab the bag in his mouth and bring it along **2 POINTS**

4. Does your dog show less interest in your own dinner preparations when the meal is one of the following vs meat-and-potato-type fare?

Vegetarian?

☐ No **NIL POINTS**

☐ Yes **1 POINT**

Vegan?

☐ No **NIL POINTS**

☐ Yes **1 POINT**

Organic, free-range, gluten-free, salt-free, antibiotic-free, wheat-free, soy-free, nut-free?

☐ No **NIL POINTS**

☐ Yes **1 POINT**

15

5. If you have a dog-friendly common space where you can let your pup off the lead, does she stay still while you unhook her (knowing that the payoff is worth it) or does she squirm and strain against the lead, meaning it will take longer to get it off?

☐ I can't get her into the dog park to begin with
NIL POINTS

☐ Flies off before I unhook her, trailing the lead behind
I POINT

☐ Waits patiently **2 POINTS**

6. Which of the following games can your dog play? Tick all that apply.

☐ Chase (i.e. fetch without the return trip) **1 POINT**

☐ Fetch **2 POINTS**

☐ Catch **3 POINTS**

☐ Football **4 POINTS**

☐ Poker **5 POINTS**

7. Does your dog understand the difference between when you go out for a short trip ('Be right back') and saying goodbye for a full day or more?

☐ It's a goodbye fit for Hollywood either way
NIL POINTS

☐ The 'Be right back' trip barely gets a head nod
I POINT

☐ He has my mobile number just in case   **2 POINTS**

19

8. Is your dog a good judge of people? If she doesn't like someone, does that person generally prove to be of weak moral character?

☐ No – she likes everyone **NIL POINTS**

☐ No – she's suspicious of everyone **NIL POINTS**

☐ She's kept me from going on several bad dates
2 POINTS

9. When your dog is cold, does she:

☐ Shiver and wait to be covered (Doggy Diva alert)
1 POINT

☐ Cuddle against you **1 POINT**

☐ Nose her way under a blanket **2 POINTS**

☐ Run to warm up **2 POINTS**

10. On a day-to-day basis, which fictional dog does yours most resemble?

☐ Pluto **NIL POINTS**

☐ Toto **1 POINT**

☐ Scooby Doo **1 POINT**

☐ Lassie **2 POINTS**

☐ Brian Griffin **2 POINTS**

Chapter Two

THE DOG ABOUT TOWN

Ah, the walk. The centre of a dog's day – other than waking up, going to sleep, eating, finding a squirrel, digging up a bone, going outside, coming home ... There's so much fun to be had, yet so many pitfalls to be on the lookout for, too. If you're interested in your dog's genius potential, you're probably way past the basic skills required to get her on the lead, keep her by your side and avoid canine combat. Hopefully your dog doesn't make walking harder – but does she actually make your life easier with her fine-tuned skills?

1. How does your dog manage the lead on a crowded pavement?

☐ Like a hungry man at a buffet **NIL POINTS**

☐ Sometimes he walks around a lamppost while I go the other way, but usually he's pretty aware **1 POINT**

☐ He navigates like a champ **2 POINTS**

2. If your dog is walking along and someone or something blocks his path suddenly, how likely is he to stop in time to avoid crashing?

☐ Crashes every time NIL POINTS

☐ Somewhat likely 1 POINT

☐ Very likely 2 POINTS

3. When you stop to wait for a light, does your dog:

☐ Strain against the lead? **NIL POINTS**

☐ Stand to perfect attention like the Queen's Guards?
2 POINTS

☐ Direct traffic? **4 POINTS**

4. If you are crossing the street and a bike is on a collision course with you, how often does your dog hesitate or otherwise register the potential danger?

☐ Never **NIL POINTS**

☐ Sometimes **I POINT**

☐ Always **2 POINTS**

Bonus for city dwellers: add 2 points to your end score if your dog has mastered the art of pretending he doesn't see the bike as urban pedestrians do.

5. Which of the following does your dog avoid on the pavement? Tick all that apply.

☐ Puddles (Doggy Diva alert) **NIL POINTS**

☐ Skateboards **I POINT**

☐ Poo (take away 2 points from your end score if he gravitates towards it instead) **2 POINTS**

☐ Wet cement **2 POINTS**

☐ Foxes **3 POINTS**

6. Would people observing you and your dog on a walk know who was walking who?

☐ Not too likely **NIL POINTS**

☐ Yes – my dog **NIL POINTS**

☐ Yes – me **2 POINTS**

7. How often does your dog get you to pull over so he can stop and smell the roses when you are clearly in a rush?

☐ I wish that was *all* he was stopping to smell
NIL POINTS

☐ He's in more of a rush than me **I POINT**

☐ They would have to be unusual roses for our climate and recent weather patterns (either that, or stained with pee)
2 POINTS

8. Does your pooch know to stay off a dog-free lawn?

☐ Yes – the lack of other dogs is the only clue she needs
I POINT

☐ Yes – if I tell her **I POINT**

☐ No. She thinks the sign reads 'Dog! Free!' and enjoys the freedom **2 POINTS**

9. How often does your dog block the way as you try to pull open a door or gate?

☐ Always **NIL POINTS**

☐ Sometimes **I POINT**

☐ I thought it said 'PUSH'! **I POINT**

☐ Never **3 POINTS**

10. Which of the following would your dog feel comfortable wearing on a walk?

☐ A bandana **1 POINT**

☐ Doggy shoes (in the ice/snow) **2 POINTS**

☐ A tutu **3 POINTS**

Chapter Three

PITCH-IN PUP

If your dog really is a superstar, he should be able to do more than simply cavort, cuddle and tuck in. To be truly happy, dog experts say, dogs need to work. Nine-tenths of British pet owners consider their dogs to be a fully fledged member of their family (and one in four owners have given their pet its own social media profile) – but does your pet pull his weight around the house, or is your pooch a bit of a mooch? Let's find out.

1. Is your dog more likely to:

☐ Eat from the rubbish bin? **NIL POINTS**

☐ Help you drag the bags to the outside bin? **1 POINT**

☐ Separate out the recycling? **2 POINTS**

2. When you are sweeping the living room, does your dog:

☐ Chase the broom around? **NIL POINTS**

☐ Eat the dust and fluff? **NIL POINTS**

☐ Hold the dustpan for you? **2 POINTS**

3. You're folding laundry on a rainy day with your pup on the couch next to you. What would you expect him to do?

☐ Take a nap ▐ NIL POINTS ▌

☐ Put on the socks ▐ I POINT ▌

☐ Help match the socks ▐ 3 POINTS ▌

4. If you ask your dog to help you mop up a spill, would she:

☐ Drink it? **I POINT**

☐ Roll around in it, using her fur to mop up the liquid?
I POINT

☐ Grab some kitchen roll? **2 POINTS**

5. Does your dog pick up his toys and put them away at the end of the day?

☐ If by 'pick up his toys and put them away' you mean sleep on my bed with his head on my pillow, then yes
NIL POINTS

☐ He'll bring me a squeaky toy if I ask nicely **1 POINT**

☐ Yes – he doesn't need to be asked **2 POINTS**

Chapter Four

HOLIDAY HOUND

Any dog in contention for genius status is certainly well behaved enough to take on holiday. But would you be forced to stay in a run-down room above a pub with (already) damp carpets or could you take him to The Ritz? Could your pup hold her own at a luxury spa or would she get you kicked out of a dog-friendly campsite? Pack your bags and let's get on our way.

1. When you are staying away from home, how quickly does your dog recognize the new base?

☐ 50/50 odds of ending up at a hog roast instead of the hotel **NIL POINTS**

☐ I trust her more than my SatNav **1 POINT**

☐ A holiday? With my dog? I probably should have skipped this section **2 POINTS**

2. Which of the following can your dog drink out of? Tick all that apply.

☐ Bowl **NIL POINTS**

☐ Water fountain **I POINT**

☐ Sprinkler **I POINT**

☐ Hose **I POINT**

☐ Champagne flute **4 POINTS**

3. Could you effectively disguise your dog as a baby in a pram and wheel him into the posh restaurant that's too chic to allow dogs?

☐ Only if Red Riding Hood were the maître d'
NIL POINTS

☐ As long as they don't serve raw meat **1 POINT**

☐ If I gave him a haircut **2 POINTS**

4. In how many languages can your dog say 'woof woof'?
Tick all that apply.

2 POINTS FOR EACH LANGUAGE

- [ ] Armenian – *haf, haf*

- [ ] Brazilian Portuguese – *au au*

- [ ] Mandarin – *wang, wang*

- [ ] French – *waouh, waouh*

- [ ] German – *rawrau, rawrau*

- [ ] Hebrew – *hau, hau*

- [ ] Spanish – *guau-guau*

- [ ] Italian – *bau, bau*

- [ ] Thai – โฮ่งโฮ่ง

- [ ] Burmese – *woke, woke*

- [ ] Other_____

5. Can your pooch respond to the command to 'Sit' in at least two languages other than English? Try it if you're not sure.

☐ No **NIL POINTS**

☐ Yes **2 POINTS**

6. In which cultural institution would your dog feel most at home?

☐ Zoo `NIL POINTS`

☐ Farm `1 POINT`

☐ Legoland `1 POINT`

☐ Art gallery `2 POINTS`

☐ Opera `3 POINTS`

7. At the Tate galleries, which piece of art would most intrigue your dog?

☐ 'The Painter and His Pug' by William Hogarth
I POINT

☐ 'Study of a Dog' by Francis Bacon **I POINT**

☐ 'Metamorphosis of Narcissus' by Salvador Dali
3 POINTS

8. Would you feel comfortable bringing your furry sidekick to a Zen garden if dogs were allowed?

☐ Not really. I'd have trouble keeping him out of the koi pond **1 POINT**

☐ He'd be less of a liability than my brother-in-law **1 POINT**

☐ Of course! He's the picture of mindfulness, always living in the moment **3 POINTS**

9. If your dog were a person, could she help you with a crossword puzzle?

☐ I'd be on my own **NIL POINTS**

☐ She'd have a fighting chance **1 POINT**

☐ Anything but the *Sunday Times'* puzzle **2 POINTS**

Ruff?

10. How well can your dog swim?

☐ I can barely get him to wade in the water at the dog-friendly pond **1 POINT**

☐ He's got a decent doggy paddle **2 POINTS**

☐ His backstroke is better than mine **4 POINTS**

Chapter Five

DO YOU SPEAK DOG?

Communication is the basis of your relationship. Your dog has to learn to speak human, and you probably even speak a little dog. Let's assess how well you've adapted to each other's native language and how well you interact non-verbally – the most important means of communication for dogs.

1. Can your dog sense when you are nervous?

☐ Not applicable – my resting state is full-blown panic attack
NIL POINTS

☐ I'd have to sweat bullets to get a reaction **I POINT**

☐ I wish my partner was half as aware of my emotional state
3 POINTS

2. To which of the following does your dog respond? Tick all that apply. I POINT FOR EACH

☐ Verbal commands

☐ Obvious hand gestures (patting your lap)

☐ The sound of a can opener

☐ Facial expressions (raised eyebrow)

☐ Sign language

☐ Subtle hand gestures (thumbs up)

☐ Stick figure drawings

3. Try to identify the number of ways in which your dog communicates. Tick all that apply.

☐ Barking

☐ Whimpering

☐ Growling (usually a warning)

☐ Putting a paw on you

☐ Trying to show you something by getting your attention through eye contact and head motions

☐ Leading you to something he wants you to see

☐ Running around in circles and yapping

☐ Howling

4. How responsive is your dog when you talk?

☐ I get a glance every now and then **1 POINT**

☐ He makes sustained eye contact **2 POINTS**

☐ He does more of the talking **3 POINTS**

5. How many words does your dog recognize?

☐ 0 **NIL POINTS**

☐ Between 1 and 5 **1 POINT**

☐ Between 6 and 10 **2 POINTS**

☐ More than 10 **3 POINTS**

6. Match the faces with the expressions.

I POINT for each correct answer

☐ Anxious

☐ On guard

☐ Ready to hunt

☐ Afraid

☐ Happy

☐ Curious

BONUS ROUND

1. Does your dog create her own abstract art?

☐ The closest she gets is climbing onto my bed with muddy paws **NIL POINTS**

☐ She expresses her creativity by digging up my flower beds **1 POINT**

☐ Give her finger paints any day, and I'd have a masterpiece for my fridge **2 POINTS**

2. Does your dog invent ways to play with non-toy items (socks, ropes, your mobile phone)?

☐ Never NIL POINTS

☐ Sometimes 1 POINT

☐ Always 2 POINTS

3. After your dog has met a new person once and knows he/she is a friend, how does she act the next time the person comes over?

☐ BFFs (I start questioning her loyalty to me)
I POINT

☐ Friendly but distant **I POINT**

☐ Appropriately happy and welcoming **2 POINTS**

4. On average, how long does it take your dog to learn a new trick?

☐ Still working on 'Stand' (he has 'Sit' covered)
NIL POINTS

☐ A week if we practise every day **I POINT**

☐ He could join the circus **2 POINTS**

5. What does 'It's a Dog's Life' actually mean? (Hint: Ask your dog!)

Chapter Six

TEST YOUR OWNER

Your dog should answer these questions himself. (Perhaps a little help from you may be required.)

1. How would your owner interpret this tail position?

☐ Submissive **NIL POINTS**

☐ Ready to take a nap **NIL POINTS**

☐ Ready to hunt **I POINT**

☐ Dominant **2 POINTS**

2. Match the faces with the expressions.

I POINT for each correct answer

☐ Anxious

☐ On guard

☐ Ready to hunt

☐ Afraid

☐ Happy

☐ Curious

3. How would you describe your owner's slippers?

☐ Fantastic chew toys `NIL POINTS`

☐ Fluffy, inert objects with little relevance to my life
`I POINT`

☐ Something I take to my owner every morning along with
the newspaper `2 POINTS`

4. Answer true or false to the following statements.

1-10: **I POINT** for each true answer
NIL POINTS for each false answer

☐ My owner has given me ample opportunity to socialize with other dogs.

☐ My owner has given me ample opportunity to socialize with those 2-legged creatures who try to shake my paw.

☐ I have been exposed to a wide variety of environments, from noisy outdoor crowds to quiet rooms where dogs should be seen and not heard.

☐ My owner is responsive to my signals.

☐ I am rewarded with positive reinforcement (petting, treats, etc.).

☐ I get a chance to exercise daily, consistent with my needs.

☐ I know what the rules are.

☐ I always get plenty of water, especially on hot days.

☐ I get the check-ups and vaccinations that I need at the vet.

☐ My owner is the alpha dog of our pack.

BONUS: My owner can do tricks on command.
Bonus: **1 POINT** for a true answer

The Activity Exam

INSTRUCTIONS

Until now I have asked you to study or interpret your dog's behaviour, or imagine what she would do in various situations. Now I'm going to ask you to actually test your dog. So make sure she has a good night's sleep (does she ever not?), dig out your stopwatch and get ready to try the activities below. You'll get the best results if you spread out the exercise over several hours or even several days to prevent testing fatigue. Hopefully your dog will have as much interest in proving her genius potential as you do (and as much at stake in the results), although somehow I doubt it. (Yet another reason to stock up on lots of her favourite treats!)

MATERIALS YOU WILL NEED

- Big and small bone (dramatically different in size)
- 3 plastic bowls
- Hurdle
- Hula hoop
- Cones
- Treats your dog loves (break them into small pieces)
- Basil (or any herb that's safe for dogs)
- Red, blue and yellow card or paper
- Plastic container with lid
- Photographs, including one of you (printed or digital)
- Computer to show video clip of *Lassie*

Hidden Treat

GOAL: to test powers of observation, spatial awareness and short-term memory.

DIRECTIONS: with your dog watching you, lay three empty bowls out on the counter. Take a dog treat and put it in one of the bowls. Tell your dog to wait as you bring the bowls down to the floor, setting them at least 30 cm apart from each other and far enough away that the dog can't see inside them. Now let your dog know he can approach the bowls. Try the experiment three times and record the results. How many times does he go immediately to the bowl with the treat?

☐ He's still looking **NIL POINTS**

☐ Once **NIL POINTS**

☐ Twice **I POINT**

☐ Three times **3 POINTS**

BONUS: take another treat, flip the bowls over and hide the treat under one, then move the bowls around for a few seconds, keeping up the appropriate chatter ('Keep your eye on the treat') as you do it. How often does your dog pick the right bowl? If all three times, add three points to your end score, or one or two as applicable.

2

Size Matters

GOAL: to test your dog's ability to learn new words.

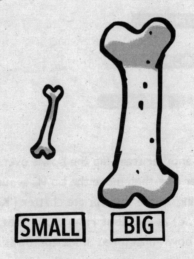

SMALL BIG

DIRECTIONS: spend a few minutes demonstrating the words 'big' and 'small' using a big and small bone. Next, lay the two bones a metre or so apart from each other and ask your dog to find the 'big' bone. This test doesn't require your dog to bring you the bone, only to indicate that he understands the word. Repeat the test three times. Did he go to the big bone?

☐ He hasn't left the couch in the past hour **NIL POINTS**

☐ Once **NIL POINTS**

☐ Twice **1 POINT**

☐ Three times **3 POINTS**

3

Doggie Olympics

GOAL: to test your dog's agility and her ability to follow directions.

DIRECTIONS: set up a simple obstacle course outside. It should have four cones (or something similar) that your dog will zigzag through, one jumpable hurdle and a hula hoop held up to jump through at the end. Ask your dog to sit and stay as you demonstrate running the course several times. Now tell your dog to get ready, get set . . . go! Did your dog:

☐ Grab the hula hoop and run? **NIL POINTS**

☐ Start off with a valiant attempt but lose focus midway? **1 POINT**

☐ Almost complete the course? **2 POINTS**

☐ Complete the course with flying colours? **3 POINTS**

4

Canine Celebrity

GOAL: to test species recognition.

DIRECTIONS: put on a video clip of *Lassie* and ask your dog to watch. Does he:

☐ Lick the screen? **I POINT**

☐ Cower under the couch? **I POINT**

☐ Bark at the screen? **2 POINTS**

☐ Attempt to imitate whatever Lassie is doing?
3 POINTS

5

Pattern Play

GOAL: to test pattern recognition

DIRECTIONS: lay out a pattern of coloured squares in this order: Red, Blue, Yellow, Red, Blue. Leave a space blank after the second blue. Point to each colour in the pattern, showing your dog Red, Blue, Yellow, Red, Blue, Blank. At the blank, ask your dog: 'What goes here? What comes after Red, Blue, Yellow, Red, Blue . . . ?' Pointing to the answers, ask your dog: 'Is it the Red Square? Blue Square? Yellow Square?' You'll have to watch your dog's signals carefully — and no prompts.

Does your dog indicate:

☐ That it's time for dinner? **NIL POINTS**

☐ Blue? **1 POINT**

☐ Red? **1 POINT**

☐ Yellow? **3 POINTS**

6

You Lookin' At Me?

GOAL: to test facial recognition.

DIRECTIONS: find a picture of yourself and four more showing other people. Make sure the faces are clear. Digital pictures are fine, too. Show your dog the pictures one by one but don't prompt him in any way. Does he whimper at the picture of you or show any recognition? Rearrange the pictures and repeat.

☐ I'm not sure he recognizes me in real life **NIL POINTS**

☐ He showed a mild interest in my picture, but only because I was eating a steak in it **1 POINT**

☐ He'd know me anywhere **3 POINTS**

7

Out-of-Reach Treat

GOAL: to test problem solving and perseverance.

DIRECTIONS: put your dog's favourite food inside a closed plastic container that he won't be able to open. Give it to him. Does he:

☐ Sit on it? **NIL POINTS**

☐ Try to open it and eventually give up? **1 POINT**

☐ Signal he would like your help to open it? **2 POINTS**

☐ Pry it open easily? **3 POINTS**

8

Sniff Test

GOAL: to test powers of detection.

DIRECTIONS: first, hide some fresh basil in the house. Next, bring your dog outside and give her a nice long whiff of one leaf of the basil. Explain that you want her to find this in the house, open the door and let her go. Does she:

☐ Run straight for her bed? **NIL POINTS**

☐ Look around for a bit then lose interest? **1 POINT**

☐ Run straight to the stash and bark when she's found it?
3 POINTS

☐ Make a caprese salad? **5 POINTS**

Analysing Your Dog's Score

Wonder Dog (140+ points)
Congratulations! Your dog is at least one furry head above the rest of the pack. His manners could get him an invitation to a Royal Ball, he soars through his day with grace, fetches every curveball, excels at problem solving, high-level communication, and even a little abstract reasoning. He knows you're the alpha dog, but in most settings – whether housekeeping, swimming or learning new languages – he outshines you. He deserves a trophy, but I can promise you he'll be happier still with a hug and a pat on the back.

Wow Bow (120–139 points)
Yes, go ahead and bow down before your dog, who has proven himself to be adaptable, eager to learn, powerfully observant, capable of handling himself in a wide variety of situations, responsive to subtle cues from you, and able to integrate new knowledge readily (particularly when it involves his next meal or squirrel chase). He'll certainly respond well if you want to teach him more, but he's already pretty close to the head of the canine class.

Clever Canine (80–119 points)
Your pooch may not jump through every hurdle and his powers of recognition may not be keen enough to get him a position with MI5, but he can certainly hold his own in most situations, responds well to strangers, seeks out new information and has proven himself highly trainable.

Fine Fido (40–79 points)
Your dog has shown some worthwhile skills in limited areas. He may not have mastered the card hustling, and he may cause a scandal if you try checking him into a fancy hotel, but he's more than capable of learning new tricks – so teach him.

Do-Over Rover (0–39 points)
Your dog will never beat you at backgammon, but he will always have your back. Not every dog was designed to be Best in Show. If you want him to impress you with his tricks, he's got a way to go. If he's savvy enough to obey basic commands, there's no need to do more, unless you want to. After all, you didn't get him to help you with quadratic equations, but he's probably very good at his essential tasks of loving, loyalty, playfulness and companionship. Still, if you hear anyone call him record-breaking, I'd check your vinyl collection ASAP.

Hopefully you got the results you wanted, and you can now brag far and wide about your dog's accomplishments. On the other hand, maybe the tests served as a wake-up call as to how much work there is ahead – for both you and your dog. If your dog listens to commands, you can give yourself much of the credit. The flip side is that the responsibility for a dog who isn't well behaved lies with the owner as well. To perform at a high level, your dog needs adequate exercise and stimulation, clear and consistent rules and boundaries, and a healthy diet. No one can perform well with a diet of junk food, no regular exercise, an erratic boss and no clear rules. You'll get hints and tips for boosting your dog's brainpower in the following section, but the good news is that you really only need to provide the basics in terms of structure, exercise and nutrition to give your pup the best chances – both in these tests and more importantly in life.

Brain Boosters

Your dog needs plenty of exercise (well over an hour a day for a big dog), healthy food and adequate stimulation. He also needs to know what the rules are and to be treated in a consistent manner. The following are a few fun ideas to boost his brainpower even further.

☐ Use any of the activity tests as exercises

☐ Teach your dog a new word each day

☐ Build a tower of blocks and ask your dog to knock it down

☐ Give your dog a pet massage to help with circulation

☐ Practise walking with a slack lead

☐ Expose your pup to a wide variety of environments: if you always take the same walk, try somewhere new; meet new people; find new parks; arrange doggy playdates; take your dog to dog-friendly households

☐ Show your dog her reflection in the mirror

☐ Play peek-a-boo

☐ Try some new holistic recipes (see *Home Cooking for Your Dog* by Christine M. Filardi. Be sure to follow her directions on transitioning to homemade food)

☐ Read books to your dog

☐ Listen to Mozart

☐ Teach your dog to paint (use non-toxic products)

☐ Set up plastic bottles and 'bowl' together

☐ Play 'basketball' by shooting balls into a basket (your dog can drop them in with his mouth)

☐ Practise commands and tricks in different settings with different distractions, gradually moving from a more- to less-controlled environment

Conclusion:

The Sound of
One Paw Clapping

I hope that you and your dog enjoyed spending time together and working through these tests and activities. At the core, these tests are meant to be fun, rather than to be taken too seriously. My editor has kindly let me take this moment to finish with a serious but brief soapbox moment on the nature of intelligence and independence. I recommend this as bedtime reading to your maverick mongrel or prima donna pooch.

As I collected data and researched this genius edition of *Test Your Dog 2*, I was struck once again by the difficulty of separating intelligence from compliance or obedience. In the eight years since the previous edition, I haven't made much progress towards figuring out how to test only or even *primarily* raw intelligence in a way that separates out environmental issues, training, temperament and a host of other factors – other than my initial statement: 'For any species, an intelligence test is context dependent'.

Studying my dog subjects the other day, I watched as some fetched toys and brought them back on command, while others ignored the toys, focusing instead on a squirrel or butterfly. Some sat down only when their bums were pushed (and popped back up again straight away), while others sat immediately with a verbal command or hand signal. Some came quickly when they were called; others ran in the opposite direction. There are signs of intelligence that factor into a dog's behaviour (figuring out how to get peanut butter out of a puzzle box or make their way through a maze), but the 'correct' behaviour is more than learning speed and capacity for complexity; it is how well they are trained, and how receptive they are to training.

A wayward dog that jets off the minute he's unhooked from his lead and jumps a fence even as the owner screams his name awkwardly across the park may be poorly trained, but he might, in the human world, be Steve Jobs or Thomas Edison. A dog who strains against his collar during his entire walk may refuse to accept reality, but so did Picasso; a dog may risk his well-being standing up to power, but so did Martin Luther King.

In humans, it occurs to me, we celebrate non-compliance,

rebelliousness or eccentricity if it is combined with genius and success. In general, though, our culture rewards compliance and values those who play expected roles.

But I'm supposed to be designing test questions so dog owners can have a laugh with their dogs during a much-needed moment of free time, not worrying about the limits of education, the dangers of high-stakes testing or of becoming a cog in a corporate machine. What was supposed to be a light read – meant primarily for fun – kept pushing me towards a profound line of inquiry. What does 'intelligence' mean? Eminent psychologist Howard Gardner explored possible ways to approach the question, starting with seven different areas of intelligence (later expanded to nine), covering everything from verbal skills to kinaesthetic skills. And it's now generally accepted that there are a range of abilities that could be called intelligence.

Further muddying the waters is the fact that many who possess a general type of all-round intelligence may not test well. Great contributions to knowledge and culture were often made by those who operated outside the 'system' and may not have been fully appreciated in their lifetimes – Vincent Van Gogh, F. Scott Fitzgerald, Mozart, to name a few. Others (Galileo) were threatened with execution. Even before that, in Ancient Greece, Plato wanted to exile all poets. Creative thinkers, those who refuse to toe the party line, have always posed a threat to power.

Again and again any test – for dogs or humans – that seems to measure intelligence has an element that rejects creative and original thinking. Where possible I have tried to design questions (albeit largely lighthearted ones) that operate outside that paradigm; exercises that assess one's ability to learn, powers of observation and problem-solving skills. Still, to perform well, the dog has to respond to our request. Does this quality alone make a dog more intelligent than one who refuses to obey? It depends on how you think about it. It is strategic to play the game in many cases, and it may set you further along towards your goals than being a rebel. But not if your true goals lie outside the climb. However, obeying humans is not only the entire basis for a dog's survival; it's literally how they were designed. Wolves that showed aggression weren't allowed to stick around to breed with the docile and compliant wolves who did. Humans gave them food and in return the wolves didn't kill them. In this deal, wolves had to repress many of their instincts, and in return they were allowed into the human pack, with its many advantages. But dogs took the deal a step further. They actually began to protect humans, even though that wasn't necessarily part of the bargain. It is just like dogs to offer so much more than was asked of them.

While I can't do more than raise questions about testing,

intelligence, original thinking and compliance, I can hopefully point us in a direction that will be productive when it comes to thinking about dogs. For a moment, instead of considering how well they performed on a test to measure their ability to fit into our world, focus on their instinctive power of survival that goes way beyond ours. As Dr Nicholas H. Dodman writes in *The Well-Adjusted Dog*, ' . . . they are especially talented in their own biological niche and would survive a lot better than us in the wild, even without a survival course'. Think about a time when your dog drew on her instincts and tried to tell you something you would never have known yourself. Maybe that a storm was on its way. Or that someone threatening was coming down the street.

One absolutely frigid winter day when I was nine months pregnant, a week before my due date, I was leaving home to pick up my nieces from daycare. As I got ready to leave, my Pitbull-Whippet, Sky, went berserk, barking, leaping up on me, almost knocking me over. I was stunned – she was a wild, high-energy dog, but she never acted like this. I've never witnessed that behaviour from her before or since. It wasn't separation anxiety – I had seen plenty of that and the signals were different. I now believe she was desperately trying to tell me something. At the time I was tired, frustrated, in a rush, and dismissed whatever it was. Later that night, when I was back at home, my waters broke. I am convinced Sky knew the baby was coming and was trying everything in her power to keep me and the baby inside where it was safe and warm. Had I listened, I wouldn't have done anything differently. Dogs can't be expected to adjust for modern medicine in their risk calculations, but we can. Still, it has stayed with me over these years as an example of the kind of canine intelligence that matters. One we should seek out more eagerly.

Bibliography

Alpha Dog, National Geographic, 2013 (DVD)

Bad Dog Season 1, Cheri Sundae Productions, 2014 (DVD)

Citizen Canine, The American Kennel Club, 2010

Dodman, Dr Nicholas H., *The Well-Adjusted Dog*, Houghton Mifflin Company, 2008

Filardi, Christine M., *Home Cooking for Your Dog: 75 Holistic Recipes for a Healthier Dog*, Stewart, Tabori & Chang, 2013

Millan, Cesar, *Be the Pack Leader*, Three Rivers Press, 2007

NOVA: Dogs and More Dogs, PBS, 2004 (DVD)

ACKNOWLEDGEMENTS

Thank you to Asher, Buddy, Max, Joe, Ivy, Mason, Jackie, Jeannine, Gemini Dogs, Echo, Lady, Ellie, Bidu, Lola, Kaiser, Bruno, the pups at Washington Square Park, my editor Caitlin for her ideas, feedback and encouragement, Rachel M., Ros, and all others who contributed to the book at Harper and of course Chuck for his brilliant illustrations. I'm grateful to Wally, too, for his wonderful brainstorms, maps and illustrations for this and many other projects. Everyone else – human and canine – you know who you are.

GCCE ⚡ AWARD

The General Certificate of Canine Excellence

This certifies that

_____

has participated in a series of tests designed to measure his/her

aptitude in respect of the following categories:

Routine skills: ☐ ☐

Neighbourhood etiquette: ☐ ☐

Pitching-in powers: ☐ ☐

Holiday helpfulness: ☐ ☐

Human communication: ☐ ☐

Knowing your owner: ☐ ☐

TOTAL GRADE ☐ ☐

EXAMINER'S SIGNATURE _____

DATE _____